VOCAL SELECTIONS FROM

ADD1NG MACHINE

A MUS1CAL

CONTENTS

NOTES FROM THE WRITERS

SONGS

Music by **JOSHUA SCHMIDT**
Libretto by **JASON LOEWITH** and **JOSHUA SCHMIDT**
Based on the play **THE ADDING MACHINE** by **ELMER RICE**

Photography by
JANNA GIACOPPO and CAROL ROSEGG

ADDING MACHINE LOGO AND LP:
by FRANK VERILIZZO / ELIRAN MURPHY GROUP

World Premiere
Recording
available on
PS Classics

For performance rights, contact:
SAMUEL FRENCH
45 West 25th Street, New York, NY 10010
(212) 206-8990
musicals@samuelfrench.com

Alfred Music Publishing Co., Inc.
16320 Roscoe Blvd., Suite 100
P.O. Box 10003
Van Nuys, CA 91410-0003
alfred.com

ISBN-10: 0-7390-5919-X
ISBN-13: 978-0-7390-5919-7

Amy Warren (Daisy)

Joe Farrell (Shrdlu)

Joel Hatch (Mr. Zero) and Jeff Still (Charles)

JASON LOEWITH, librettist

Adding Machine: A Musical is the culmination of a thirteen-year artistic crush. Back in 1994, my first boyfriend introduced me to the world of opera. I'd known the classic repertoire—as a young theater artist, I was already inculcated into the golden age of Rodgers and Hammerstein, and recognized that Sondheim would forever be an influence on my work—but what really rocked my world was a trio of compositions: Vaughan Williams' *Riders to the Sea*, which set Synge's play to music, nearly word for word; Adams' *Nixon in China*, which blew me away with its grand theatricality and Alice Goodman's tour-de-force libretto; and Kurt Weill's *Street Scene*, based on the play by Elmer Rice.

The latter so fascinated me that I started reading every Rice play I could find, and when I came across *The Adding Machine*, I was startled. Rice wrote socio-political work with a *rhythm*, a theatrical language that soared above stale naturalism. The play's first scene—Mrs. Zero's four-page, uninterrupted harangue against her husband—screamed *opera aria* to me. And that's how it began.

A series of failed attempts at finding composers ensued during the next few years, punctuated by a rejected application to the NEA in 1994 (they relented twelve years later, and funded the project). I drafted my idea for the office scene, plus a couple of more bits and pieces. It wasn't until I became the artistic director of Chicago's Next Theatre in 2002 that everything started falling into place. And thankfully so: at age 26, I was hardly ready to write the piece, and the composers I'd approached were the wrong collaborators anyway. So the idea lay fallow for many years.

In 2004, I met the intense and strangely brilliant composer Josh Schmidt, who had been writing incidental music for theater in the Midwest. His score for an adaptation of *Crime and Punishment* at Writers' Theatre in Glencoe so enthralled me that I asked him to design the music and sound for a production of Caryl Churchill's play *Far Away*. We hit it off so well—and my theater was just on the verge of being financially stable enough to produce a world premiere—that I off-handedly asked whether he'd read this play, which I had a crazy idea for musicalizing. I told him about the four-page aria that I heard in my head, my passion for the play's dark exploration of the American Dream, my ideas for the work's dramaturgical structure, and the twenty or so pages I'd written years before. To my utter astonishment, Josh was on board… and a couple of months later, he showed up with my aria. Well, *his* aria. I'd had Sondheim's lighthearted comic masterpiece "Getting Married Today" (from his groundbreaking 1970 musical *Company*) in my head; Josh brought me a musical hellscape from the world of Hieronymus Bosch: grotesque, angular, hateful, disturbed. As an artist, I was speechless; as a producer, I was terrified.

But our director for *Far Away*, Lisa Portes, had once told me that fear was a good sign in our business, so I asked Josh what else he had. He played me the sweet spot of what would become Scene Six: "Daisy's Confession" in the Elysian Fields, a simple, earnest and enthralling melody that cried "yearning" more clearly than any piece of music I had ever heard before. It was the opposite of the first scene. When Josh told me his vision for the piece was a progression from Mrs. Zero's manic aria to the unsullied sweetness of "Daisy's Confession," I knew that I had finally found the right partner.

The help of literally hundreds of people and supporters followed, but none of them played so vital a role as that of our director, David Cromer, who leapt aboard after our first workshop and became the essential third wheel we needed to provide the friction, angst, and misery that we needed. Cromer's contributions to the piece's dramaturgy were wonderful, and his vision for the staged result (as anyone who saw it will tell you) was extraordinary. I am not sure I will ever again experience as complete an artistic success as *Adding Machine: A Musical*, but I am convinced it will not happen without collaborators as smart, talented, and invested as Josh Schmidt and David Cromer.

There were, of course, some moments of extreme delight in the process. For example, the office scene gelled magically in a workshop rehearsal, despite our doubts. Or, when Josh asked for a Tin-Pan Alley love song, the lyrics to "I'd Rather Watch You" flew out of my head. I'll never forget fighting tears, listening to spontaneous applause for "Mr. Zero's Confession," which is Josh's most personal and extraordinary accomplishment in this remarkable score. Or Cromer's hard-won triumph: the dancing jail cells during "Didn't We?" He knew better than any of us how to release just the right amount of "funny" into this airless piece. It all came together (well, most of it anyway) at our first preview in the winter of 2007, when we realized we'd written a pitch-black musical comedy. I was cornered by a board member that night; he'd seen the workshop two years ago and had serious doubts, but this result left him limp as a dishrag. So I asked him, "What else do you expect when you get three nebbishy egomaniacal losers to put on a musical about a nebbishy egomaniacal loser? Of course it works!"

JOSHUA SCHMIDT, composer and co-librettist

One could say that the "Machine" chose me first, and then I
chose it. Adapting Elmer Rice's 1923 expressionist juggernaut
was the long-time dream of librettist Jason Loewith. Apparently,
he had approached other composers with the project to no avail.
When he finally inquired as to my interest in January 2004, I
was working as Sound Designer on a show he was producing
at the Next Theatre Company in Evanston, Illinois, where
he served as Artistic Director. Up to that point, I had never
written a musical, nor did I envision myself writing one. I knew
of Elmer Rice—his play *Street Scene* had been wonderfully
adapted into a musical theatre piece by Kurt Weill and Langston
Hughes—but up to that point, I had not read, seen, or even heard of *The Adding Machine.*

I certainly was no stranger to musical theatre; I had years of experience as an accompanist and
rehearsal pianist behind me, and spent my early years slumming around the halls of the Skylight Opera
in Milwaukee, Wisconsin. I possessed a broad knowledge of musical theatre and opera repertoire,
and musical theatre was the medium through which I passed into composing and sound designing for
theatre and dance. Alas, somewhere between then and 2004, my interest in musicals faded a bit as I
became increasingly more active in contemporary music and composition, electronic music, jazz, and
rock and roll. Within this music I still found the challenge, the surprise, and the edge that seemed to
elude me in new musicals, and I possessed no interest in reliving or adhering to classic book musical
structure and song form because, frankly, it had been done many times over, and many times better than
I think I could ever recreate. So, I found occupational happiness in the eclecticism and adventure of
writing all sorts of things in all sorts of styles for all sorts of plays and dance projects.

Yet, here I was, a 27-year-old composer and sound designer with few, if any, significant credits to my
name outside of the Milwaukee/Chicago area, being presented with my first commission. Jason told
me that if I finished it, the Next Theatre would produce it. Maybe—*if* it was good. This was not to be a
high-paying gig…

I didn't hesitate. I said yes. I committed to the project.

Then, I read it....

Nothing about the play seemed to radiate anything conventional. Two of the first four scenes were
long, expansive, near-circular monologues by seemingly unlikable characters in unfortunate situations.
The other characters seemed equally challenged. In glancing at the first production credits, I noticed
that nearly thirty actors had been required for its initial realization. Each scene seemed to be a stylistic
juxtaposition to the one preceding it, with adjunct scenic shifts that were equally eccentric. The density
in which Rice meditated upon the meaning of human life, criss-crossing socialism with reincarnation,

Taylorism, xenophobia, the urban experience, love, and technology seemed at times impossible to penetrate.

Mind you, the play, as written, would have never fit into the cozy confines of Next Theatre, which possesses a hodgepodge of the barest essentials of technical theatre infrastructure on a shoe-string budget. Shortly after accepting the gig, I was working on another show in Chicago, and told another member of that project about my new commission. He flat out told me that he never went to see anything at Next because he hated the space, he felt it to be impossible to design anything interesting in there, and that what I was being asked to do was an impossible, stupid idea that would never work.

That's when I became convinced that I had a good thing on my hands.

Not to say that things effortlessly rolled onto the page, because nothing could be further from the truth. The initial stages of the development of the piece involved Jason and I doing extensive cutting and redacting of the text, compressing two scenes into a wholly new one, cutting characters down to be convincingly realized by nine performers, fretting about what orchestration would work for the piece, figuring out how to fit in the space—and not bankrupt the theatre. We split the initial adaptation duties, with Jason taking the "Office" and "Party" scenes, and compressing Rice's original fifth and sixth scenes into a new "Jail" scene. I started with the "Bed" scene and then moved on to the "Elysian Fields," with the "Courtroom" scene to follow. All of these things needed to be considered, because adapting this show for this space meant confronting the practicalities of production during the writing process, and not after.

One of the great things about Elmer Rice's text that suited my interests and abilities was its eclecticism. With my formal training as a composer of new music (as opposed to theatre music), my wide range of musical interests and experience, and my short-yet-obsessive attention span, I had become a "jack-of-all-trades, master-of-none" composer. I never was able to commit or devote myself to anyone particular style like classical, rock, or jazz because I would eventually get bored and hunger for something different. For me, the theatre became a perfect environment to embrace and experience all that interested me in a practical way. To survive, I had to become adept enough in my knowledge and skills to write and produce music, whether live or recorded, in any style, at any time relative to the needs of a greater project. *Adding Machine: A Musical* proved no different, although this time I could finally explore where my own compositional voice resided, considering the influences of John Cage, Morton Feldman, Henry Cowell, George Antheil, Luigi Russollo, Johannes Brahms, Erik Satie, Igor Stravinsky, Terry Riley, Richard Rodgers, Steve Reich, Wayne Shorter, Kurt Weill, George Gershwin, Tom Waits... the list goes on and on. In the end, I did not want to produce a "stylistic grab-bag" of a piece, but a fully-formed, personally voiced new entity. Style has never interested me. I have never been a stylish kinda guy. Besides, I can never keep up with trends, and it is easier being "un-hip". Furthermore, I have always wished that the concept of musical genre was invisible—that we, as listeners, would never let an industry-given genre label interfere or influence how we respond to what we hear.

Incidentally, my three favorite musical theatre experiences prior to the inception of *Adding Machine* all revolved around small, intimate settings. The first musical I ever saw was Leonard Bernstein's *Candide*—in a converted mechanic's garage that was home to the Skylight Opera for nearly three decades before they moved to better digs. They had sets positioned in unexpected places, people flying around everywhere, and a whole orchestra crammed into what seemed like closet space. It was magical, simply because it had to be. Conversely, I worked on productions of *The Fantasticks* and *Jacques Brel Is Alive and Well and Living in Paris*, which hinge completely on the material and not extravagant splendor. Now, I have worked on some real spectacles in my days in the theatre—in big venues with big budgets—but for me personally, none equal the charm or power of those experiences felt in the friendly confines of a small theatre storefront.

The first music written for *Adding Machine* was "Daisy's Confession." This was before I met my wife; in my single years, tortured romantic that I was. I rewrote and re-orchestrated that song for a long time; kept it secret, even. There are some difficult and explosive emotional moments in Rice's play, but I have always felt that the act of openly articulating your love for another person without a net when you have never, ever done so before in your life is maybe the most profoundly frightening thing many normal people ever experience.

Later on, *after* I met the woman I was to eventually marry (Amy Martinez-Miller, for those who want to know), I wrote "I'd Rather Watch You" while sitting and having lunch at the Next Theatre administrative offices, bothering people while they worked, as is my usual modus operandi. I was in love, of course, and I had just watched Sergio Leone's masterful film *Once upon a Time in America*, which uses the old song "Amapola" to great effect in an otherwise violent bloodbath of a movie. I love such juxtapositions and love them in my work. Sometimes they work and sometimes they don't, yet, I really never seem to care enough to stop trying. I think this song works; and it makes me think about when I met my wife… on a street corner... in Brooklyn.

Not long after receiving the commission, I caught an original musical review at Martyr's on Lincoln called *Fatty Arbuckle's Spectacular Musical Review and Melancholy Play*. Performing a few of the songs was the spectacular Amy Warren. Right then and there, I knew who would be singing these songs. I walked up to her afterwards and told her I was writing a musical, and that she would be in it. I believe she thought I was crazy.

The first song I presented to Jason was "Something to Be Proud Of,"—which I was convinced would get me booted off the project. The piece did scare him a little, and he reminded me that it might be a good idea not to scare too many people away with the rest of the music. I agreed with and understood his concern, but, as I would say to him (and later broadcast to the masses on National Public Radio), we were adapting Elmer Rice's *The Adding Machine*, and not *Chitty, Chitty, Bang, Bang*. Jason, being a wonderful collaborator, did not fire me.

Incidentally, I had no one in mind for the role of Mrs. Zero. I only knew that it was probably hard to sing, and that any time "normal" people see any time signature other than 4/4 or 3/4, they get scared. Cyrilla Baer won the role in audition, and actually, her fearless performance took that song further than I ever imagined it.

Another story about this song: I had worked with director David Cromer a few times prior to 2004. Each time I worked with him, I became a better sound designer. Through this, we have become good friends, and I trust him implicitly. Few people have ever pushed me harder to achieve more. He became my first choice to direct this project after he saw an early workshop of the piece, then took me to a bar and told me everything I was doing wrong and would need to change. He took out the workshop program and showed me sketches of what the first three scenes of the play should look like, including staging the first scene in an upright bed. I brought the idea of David directing the show to Jason. After fully vetting the situation for about six months (it is a hard thing to give up your child, especially to someone as intense as David Cromer), he agreed. It was one of the smartest administrative moves either of us made in the course of building this show.

At one point, during another workshop of this show, David (now the director) leaned back in his seat, pushed his glasses back towards his brow, and told me, "Josh, I may be a stupid person, but I am also *very* smart. There is *tremendous* value in this observation. If you do not cut the air out of this song and make it go faster, I will lose interest after two minutes." Startled, I cut three minutes out of the original version. It was like squeezing water out of solid rock; nevertheless, this direction made "Something to Be Proud Of" the hell-raising six minute opening number it is now.

From this, one can conclude that creating successful musicals seldom happens in a vacuum. I, personally, need people to challenge and deepen my ideas; otherwise, how could they ever withstand public scrutiny? Such collaboration does not occur without a certain level of pain and stress over long periods of time. One aspect that took two productions to solve was the character of Shrdlu. Jason's original concept was that Shrdlu sings a gospel song in jail, and then in heaven, he sings the blues. Just what the arc of this character did was not clear until we released him of his burdens with the song "Freedom" (which Zero later reprises in the last scene). "The Gospel According to Shrdlu" is the beginning of this journey, and its inclusion within the jail scene reflects what we, as collaborators, saw in the humor and absurdity of Rice's brilliant writing.

Within the absurdity of the jail scene comes what may be the most ironically tender ballad in the show: "Didn't We?" To me, it constitutes my favorite aspects of Brahms, Sondheim, and Burt Bacharach etched into one. Within its orchestration (which I prefer to do as I write, and not after—composition *is* orchestration), my attachment to the economy of musical gesture is the most clearly expressed. No melody wanted to seem wasted—it is the closest I got to pure counterpoint. With this song, the most unlikely of songs, David Cromer unleashed his idea for a dance number: Mrs. Zero dancing with Mr. Zero, as he carries his jail cell. In an earlier draft of the score, the cymbal whooshes followed the phrase structure, until such time as our sound designer Tony Smolenski IV pointed out that one of them should be shifted by one bar to accompany the lifting of the jail cell. I took his note. In fact, I took every musical note Tony gave me. For that matter, I took every musical note that anyone gave me, or at least tried to. Happily. It takes a village, as they say.

Of all the songs in the show, "Zero's Confession" is probably the number that I am most attached to. It took me a year-and-a-half of just staring at the original Rice text wondering, "How the hell do I write a musical number eight minutes long for a guy named Mr. Zero? How does a guy like that sing?" A year-and-a-half. As a piece of music, it operates like something Benjamin Britten might write—if he liked the band Fugazi. At many points during this piece, Mr. Zero, the chorus, and each pit instrument (piano, synthesizer, percussion) are playing something completely different and melodically independent from each other. Yet, the text, along with the stunning performance of Joel Hatch (one of my favorite actors to work with in Chicago, for whom I always intended to write the role) drove this song forward with vicious energy and poignant sadness that surprised me every night I watched him sing it.

Many people in Chicago and New York (regardless of what they thought of the piece) told me that they had seldom seen a theatrical piece so integrated from the ground up—all of it , including lights, sets, costumes, sound, music, script, direction, production, and performances. I do not know how that happened. Perhaps it was just the right time for this project, an experience that everyone seemed to get on board with and give all of their attention and care. For that, I am eternally grateful, and isn't that how the theatre should be?

SOMETHING TO BE PROUD OF

Lyrics by
JASON LOEWITH and
JOSHUA SCHMIDT

Music by
JOSHUA SCHMIDT

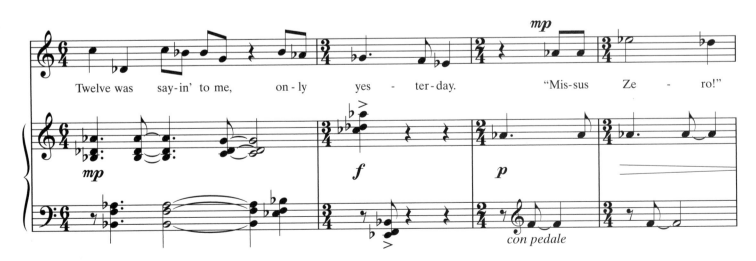

14

Safety

16

C

Something to Be Proud Of - 22 - 5
32158

Nine was say-in' to me, "Mis-sus Ze - ro!" Mis-sus

Ze - ro. Mis - ter

Ze - ro. Mis - ter

Nine was say-in' to me, on-ly yes-ter-day. "Mis-sus Ze - ro!"

Ze - ro, Mis - ter Ze - ro.

Ze - ro, Mis - ter Ze - ro.

20

24

26

do with - out_____ her?

ff

Mrs. Zero:

I   was   a   fool!_____

mp   **sffz**   **p**   **sffz**

con pedale

_____ A   fool   for   mar - ry - ing   you!_____

___ I   did - n't   pick   much   when   I   picked_   you!_____

30

Something to Be Proud Of - 22 - 19
32158

Chorus & Mrs. Zero:

I was a fool!_____ A fool for

Mrs. Zero:

mar - ry - ing you!_____ I did - n't pick much when

Chorus:

I picked_ you!_____ You ain't much to be proud

of! She was a fool!_____ A

M **Mrs. Zero:**

mar - ry - ing you._____ I did - n't pick much when

I picked_ you._____ You ain't much to be proud_____

_ of._____

I'D RATHER WATCH YOU

Lyrics by
JASON LOEWITH and
JOSHUA SCHMIDT

Music by
JOSHUA SCHMIDT

ZERO'S CONFESSION

Lyrics by
JASON LOEWITH and
JOSHUA SCHMIDT

Music by
JOSHUA SCHMIDT

42

out of ten e - nough! _____ Six and

six makes twelve, and five, that's sev - en - teen. Add

eight, that's twen - ty - five! That's twen - ty - five years! Eight

hours a day each day ex - cept Sun - days. One

fig - gers   in - side   my   head._____   I've

fig - gered   them   out   of - ten   e - nough!_____

D

_____   But   who   wants   one   week   with__   the   wife   yell-in'

senza pedale

where   to__   get   off!   And   don't   for - get   New   Years',__

sfz   *sfz*   *mf*

sfz   *senza pedale*

48

52

straight through her win - dow! Noth - in' else on! And

I told the cops 'cause the wife would-n't leave me a - lone!

H (♩ = ♩.)

Wom - en! They get a - way with mur -

der! I've seen lots of birds that I'd like to grab, but I

molto pedale

J **Presto** ♩ = 160

one time last sum-mer, I fired that pop bot-tle in a crowd at the

Po - lo Grounds! *And ev-'ry-one was yel - lin'...*

K *pp*
Chorus:

poco a poco accel.

Kill the Um - pire! Kill the Um - pire! Kill the Um - pire! Kill the Um - pire! Kill the Um - pire!

Presto ♩ = 160   **Mr. Zero:** *ffff*

Vamp
repeat 6-10 times

Kill the Um - pire! Kill the Em - pire! Kill the Em - pire! Kill the...

58

DIDN'T WE

Lyrics by
JASON LOEWITH and
JOSHUA SCHMIDT

Music by
JOSHUA SCHMIDT

Rubato (♩ = 76)

Mrs. Zero:

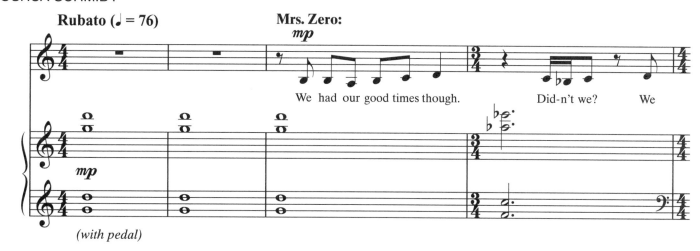

We had our good times though. Did-n't we? We

had our highs 'long with the lows. Did-n't we?___ Did-n't we? Those

days___ at the beach, and that trip to the fair! And our nights at the

Mr. Zero:

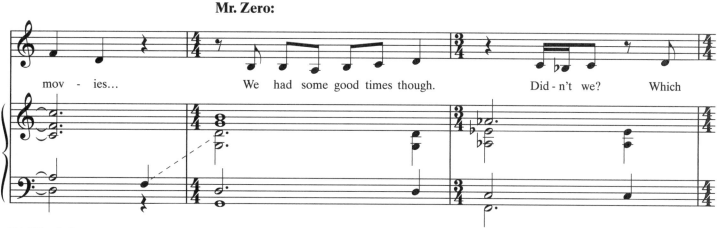

mov-ies... We had some good times though. Did-n't we? Which

Didn't We - 5 - 1
32158

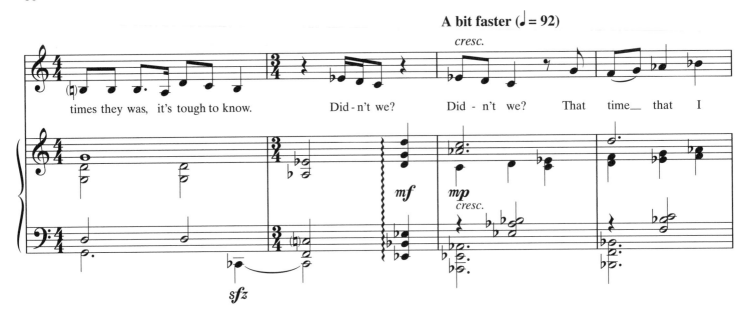

61

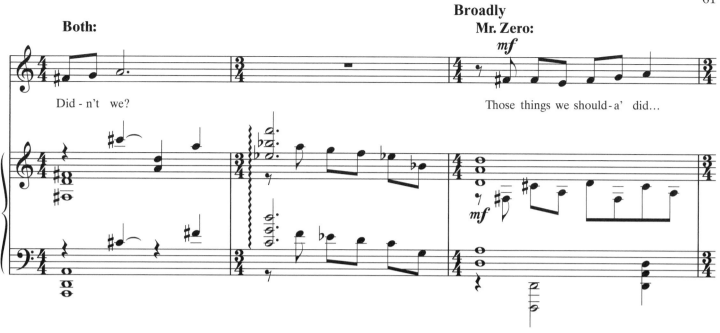

Didn't We - 5 - 3
32158

62

Didn't We - 5 - 4
32158

THE GOSPEL ACCORDING TO SHRDLU

Lyrics by
JASON LOEWITH and
JOSHUA SCHMIDT

Music by
JOSHUA SCHMIDT

Freely (♩ = 112)

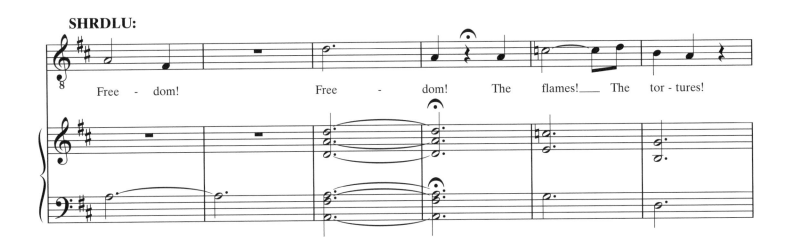

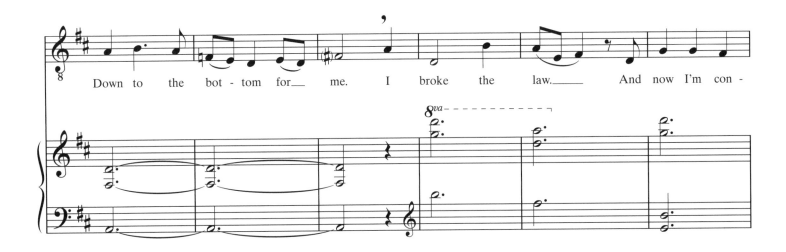

The Gospel According to Shrdlu - 9 - 1
32158

SHRDLU: (spoken) "I am the foulest, the most sinful
of murderers. You only murdered your employer, Mr. Zero.
But I? I murdered my mother."

ZERO: "The hell you say!"

demned.

Adagio con rubato

SHRDLU: (spoken) "She was a saint, I tell you, a saint.
She cared for me and watched over me as only a mother can."

"From my infancy, she devoted herself
to putting me on the right path."

p

"She taught me to be thrifty, devout, unselfish, to shun evil companions
and to shut my eyes and ears to all temptations of the flesh."

Cue: "In short, to become a virtuous,
respectable, and God-fearing man…"

Vamp if necessary

last time only

And

Vivace (♩ = 136)

SHRDLU: (spoken) "We're sinners, Mr. Zero, you and me."

what be - comes of mor - al - i - ty?

mf   rall.

The Gospel According to Shrdlu - 9 - 2
32158

"And as sinners, we deserve punishment. And punishment eventually will come. And when it comes, it will be horrible."

"And it will be just."

"That fatal Sunday, Dr. Amaranth,…"

"…our minister, was having dinner with us."

"One of the few pure spirits left on this earth."

Andante con rubato (♩ = c. 96)

We said grace._____ And ev-'ry-thing was go-ing a-long_ as

mf

us-u-al. Dis-cuss-ing the ser-mon, just like ev-'ry oth-er

DAISY'S CONFESSION

Lyrics by
JASON LOEWITH and
JOSHUA SCHMIDT

Music by
JOSHUA SCHMIDT

74

Daisy's Confession - 13 - 2
32158

Faster (♩ = c. 144)

home,   all   the way   home._____

I   felt   like   kiss - in'

ped. ad lib.

you,_____   but   I   did - n't have the

cresc.

Wish - in' 'bout no - bod - y else but you!____

nerve,____ the nerve._____   I felt like

cresc.

80

let you____ all you want-ed.____ An' I ain't had the

nerve to tell you be - fore!____ I know it

would - a' been wrong,_____ but I was - n't think - in' 'bout

Moderato
($\quad$ = c. 108)

p

you.   I

freely   *rit.*

Oh!_____ Dai - sy,   if I   on - ly   knew...

rit.

did - n't have noth - in' to live for with you   gone.

p

mp

Why would I want to go on liv - in'____ for?_____ I

mp

Dai - sy,   how

84

Daisy's Confession - 13 - 12
32158

FREEDOM!
(Reprise)

Lyrics by
JASON LOEWITH and
JOSHUA SCHMIDT

Music by
JOSHUA SCHMIDT

Moderato con rubato ($\quad$ = 108)

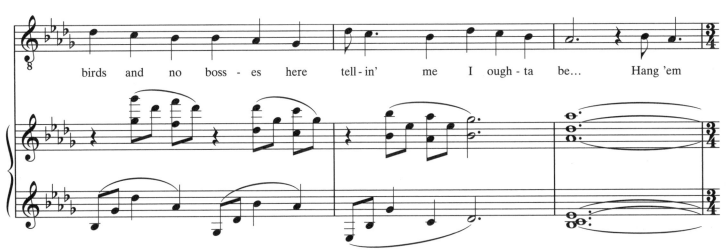

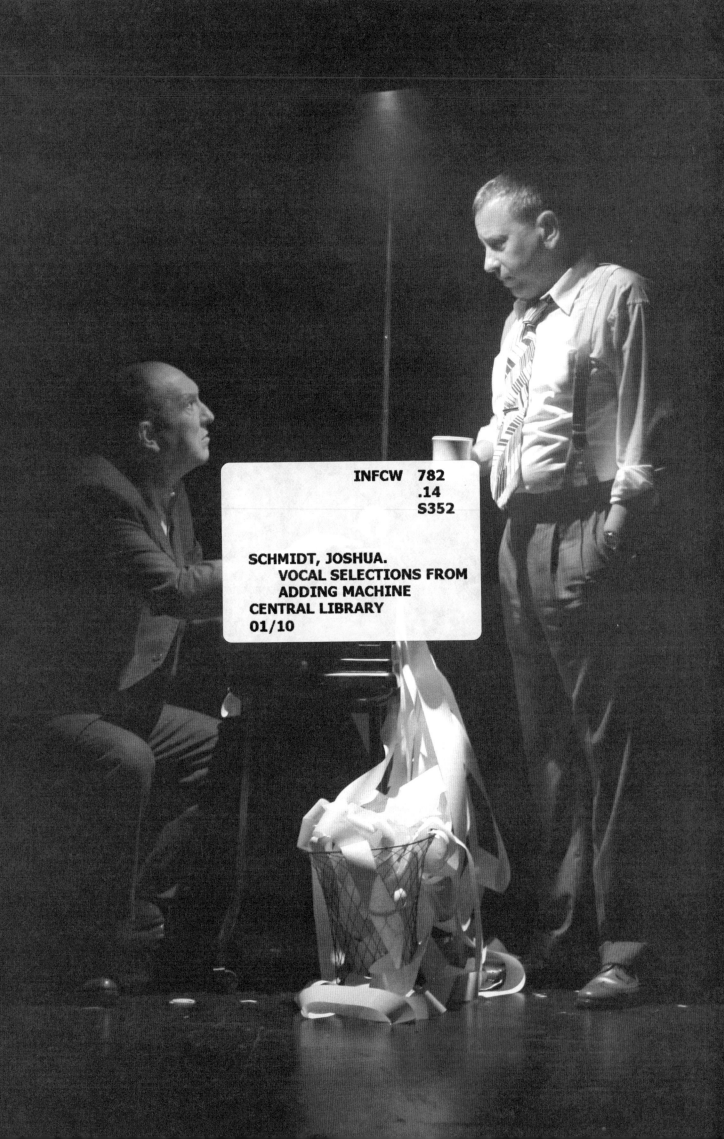